A PORTFOLIO OF

LIGHTING
IDEAS

CREATIVE
PUBLISHING
international

MINNETONKA, MINNESOTA

www.howtobookstore.com

CONTENTS

© Copyright 1996
Creative Publishing international, Inc.
5900 Green Oak Drive
Minnetonka, Minnesota 55343
1-800-328-3895
www.howtobookstore.com

President/CEO: David D. Murphy
Executive V.P./Editor-in-Chief: Patricia K. Jacobsen
Vice President/Retail Sales & Marketing: Richard M. Miller

Author: Home How-To Institute™
Creative Director: William B. Jones
Associate Creative Director: Tim Himsel
Group Executive Editor: Paul Currie
Managing Editor: Carol Harvatin
Editors: Mark Biscan, Jon Simpson
Art Directors: Ruth Eischens, Gina Seeling
Copy Editor: Janice Cauley
Vice President of Development
    Planning & Production: Jim Bindas
Production Coordinator: Laura Hokkanen

Printed by R.R. Donnelly & Sons Co.
10 9 8 7 6 5 4 3 2

Library of Congress
Cataloging-in-Publication Data
Portfolio of Lighting Ideas
p. cm.

ISBN 0-86573-963-3 (softcover)
1. Lighting, Architectural and decorative 2. Interior decoration
I. Cy DeCosse Incorporated.
NK2115.5.L5P67 1996
729'.28—dc20
95-40811

Front cover photos (top to bottom) courtesy of Homes
by Timberpeg, Russ Chapple photographer Gencorp,
Schonbek World Wide Lighting Inc. Back cover photos
(top to bottom) courtesy of Interlubke and Pittsburg
Corning Corp.

Background photos this page, and pages 52-53, 54, 58,
66, 72, 78, 84 & 90 courtesy of Tynsdale, a division of
Frederick Cooper Lamps

Photo courtesy of Lindal Cedar Homes, Inc., Seattle, Washington

(above) **Natural light** streams in through tall windows and bounces off the bright white walls, glass block and high ceilings. At night, wall sconces and a pendant-style ceiling light change the lighting in the room, creating an intimate setting with dramatic shadows.

(right) **Large cathedral windows** and soaring skylights fill the vaulted ceiling with lots of natural light, creating a grand lighting scheme in keeping with the architecture.

Photo courtesy of Homes by Timberpeg

Pretty and practical, this bathroom mirror ensemble includes fluorescent lights along each side for optimum makeup application, and small recessed lights across the top for general lighting.

WHAT MAKES GREAT LIGHTING?

Lighting your home both beautifully and effectively has never been easier. Thoughtfully planned lighting can create a number of unique effects throughout a room, as well as make your home a comfortable and attractive place to live.

There have been dramatic changes in the last 10 to 15 years in the way people plan and execute their home lighting schemes. More than ever before there is a greater selection of fixtures and lighting equipment. A custom lighting plan can be created to suit every interior, taste and budget.

Combining various lighting techniques and effects can create a number of different moods and atmospheres in a room. Even an ordinary table lamp, and the type of shade used, will have an impact on the the type of light created and the mood of a room.

For an interior lighting plan to be successful it takes time and careful preplanning. Even though it is easier to settle for an overhead fixture and a couple of lamps than to deal with special wiring requirements or window placement, the extra time and effort are well worth it. This important step is often forgotten or given minimal attention.

When planning the lighting for your home, you should consider what the functions of the room will be, and who will be using it. Flexible lighting is essential in the dining room, where a chandelier may be elegant, but too bright unless a dimmer switch is used to soften the mood. Placing a chandelier off-center or over the buffet makes a room appear larger, while valance or cove lighting, recessed fixtures and over-the-buffet spotlights supplement this general light source. Use accent lighting in the living room to highlight glassware or art.

The lighting plan for a family room or den should be similar to the living room, with greater emphasis on direct light for games, hobbies and desk work. If the room includes a computer, you can avoid reflections by choosing a fixture with baffles, such as an adjustable pendant lamp.

Bedrooms need a wide range of general lighting ranging from soft for relaxing, to bright for cleaning, all easily controlled with a simple dimmer switch. A shared bedroom should have separate task lights, such as bedside lamps or adjustable track lights above the headboard for reading. In a child's room, ceiling or wall fixtures are a better choice than portable lamps, which are easily broken. In baths, light for safety, and eliminate shadows with fixtures on both sides of grooming mirrors. Kitchens need multipurpose lighting for efficiency as well as task lighting for activities such as food preparation, and ambient, or background, lighting for activities like dining.

Natural light streams in through two round-top windows and brings light deep into the corners of this bedroom. At night, light for reading and other tasks is provided by a table lamp and floor lamp.

A glass block wall and ceiling-mounted spotlights add sparkle to this elegant dining area.

Planning

CHOOSING THE RIGHT LIGHT

Lighting aids us as we go about our daily lives. It helps us with specific tasks and provides general illumination for safety and convenience. In a successful lighting plan, each fixture has a specific role that contributes to the safety and comfort of a room. The way you combine these fixtures affects the overall lighting scheme and influences the effect of light as a design tool.

Light enhances or changes the perception of a room. It creates moods and highlights focal points. Lighting can give a room an air of formality or a casual feel. Because the influence of natural light on a room changes as the sun moves across the sky, the interplay of natural and artificial light is constantly changing over the course of a day. Observe these changes to get an idea of how your lighting needs will change so you can plan a lighting scheme to accommodate them.

The most effective way to add dramatic accent lighting is with a well-coordinated mix of lights. Combinations of different types of lighting can be used to highlight various features of a room, from ornate architecture to a treasured art collection. Ceiling- or wall-mounted track lights or spotlights can be directed downward onto a sculpture or paintings. They can also work in reverse, beaming up from the floor to accent the features.

General illuminators, such as ceiling fixtures, track lighting, or pendant fixtures, should be teamed with task lights directed onto counters and cooktops. In entries and hallways, lighting should ensure safety first, but it can also be used to add drama. Three or four elegant wall sconces, mounted on the wall going up a stairway, make more sense than a hard-to-clean hanging fixture over the landing.

Once your plan for general lighting has been formed, think about where you'd like to add task or accent lighting. General lighting, such as luminous ceiling fixtures, track lights, or pendant fixtures, can be used with task lights directed at specific work areas, such as counters and cooktops, without affecting the overall lighting in a room. In entryways and hallways, the function of lighting is safety first, but it can also be used to add a dramatic effect or enhance a design theme.

Table lamps are the simplest way to add accent lighting to a setting. Lamps supply task lighting at the end of a sofa or beside a chair. When placed on a low table, lamps create warm accent lighting and come in styles to suit almost any decor.

(top) A chandelier adds ambient light and elegance to the dining room and complements the table setting.

(right) This traditional table lamp, with its fabric shade, produces a soft, diffused light that's perfect for reading because it doesn't glare in your eyes.

Natural daylight comes in through large windows and is reflected around the room by the large mirror over the mantel. At night the mood of this simple sitting room changes dramatically when illuminated by simple table lamps, a fire and candlelight.

Table lamps work well in corners, on a low table in the center of the room or behind tall plants with the light shining through the leaves to make an attractive pattern on the ceiling. If you plan to include lights that plug in, mark these in the same layout as the table lamps, since outlets will be needed for these as well.

Table lamps need outlets, so plan accordingly when deciding placement. Mark your layout where you would like to use them. Lamps intended to be positioned away from the walls should be plugged into floor outlets. A floor outlet is sunk into the floor and covered with a flap when not in use. Installing floor outlets is safer than trailing cords across the room.

Following some general guidelines will help you design the most effective and efficient lighting plan for your personal needs. For example, recessed fixtures should be spaced 6 to 8 feet apart for general lighting, and flood bulbs

should be used. For task lighting, the fixtures should be installed 15 to 18 inches apart.

Pendant lights and chandeliers should be hung so the bottom of the fixture is about 30 inches above the table. If the fixture has a bare bulb and open bottom, it should be hung low enough to avoid shining light in the user's eyes.

The diameter of a hanging light should be at least 1 foot less than the diameter of the table underneath it. Beside a chair or next to a bed, a hanging light should be positioned with its lower edge about 4 feet from the floor. For lighting over a desk, the lower edge of a fixture should sit about 15 inches above the desktop.

Short floor lamps, 40 to 42 inches high, should line up with your shoulder when you're seated. Tall lamps should be set about 15 inches to the side, and 20 inches behind the center of the book you're reading. The bottom of a table lamp should be at eye level when you are seated.

A good lighting scheme takes into account the activities a room is used for. Each room needs a different type of lighting plan, one that provides the proper light for activities such as eating, working or entertaining. A second function of a good lighting scheme is to create a pleasant and enhancing atmosphere.

The living room requires a number of different types of lighting because of the range of activities that take place there. Soft, general lighting from indirect sources, such as wall sconces, table lamps, recessed fixtures or cove lighting should be sufficient for relaxing, entertaining, and watching television.

Lighting used to accent objects should be at least three times brighter than the general lighting. Spotlights, table lamps and floor lamps are good sources of direct light for reading. Use accent lighting to focus on a favorite furniture grouping, wash a wall of artwork with soft light or focus a spotlight on an important furniture piece, such as an armoire.

Dining rooms are used primarily for entertaining, and lighting is an important part of entertaining. From a casual card game to a full-scale formal dinner party— lighting adds atmosphere to every occasion. Including a dimmer switch allows you to easily adjust the light for the various functions and activities.

Lighting in the kitchen has to look good and work hard. Kitchens need

An intricate crystal chandelier sets the stage for a classical evening and adds the crowning touch of elegance to this formal setting.

subtle, ambient light for dining as well as task light for work areas. Spotlights can create both functional task and background lighting.

In bedrooms, the main source of light is ambient, or general, lighting; it sets the tone for the room. Task lighting is needed for dressing, storage and reading. Decorative accent lighting can be incorporated into the general lighting scheme.

Bathrooms require functional lighting for fast showers and personal preparation. For a more soothing effect, consider taking advantage of the glass and mirrors to create a relaxing atmosphere.

The bright glare of natural morning sunlight is diffused and softened by a sheer lace curtain. A bedside table lamp provides enough task lighting for nighttime reading.

Lofty cathedral windows and large round-top casement windows make maximum use of the natural light available to this room.

Design
TYPES OF LIGHTING

Because your rooms are used for a variety of functions, each requires a different combination of lighting types. You need task lighting to read or work by, ambient background light to make the environment more comfortable, and decorative or accent lighting to add focus and drama to interior design schemes. The chemistry of these combinations varies from room to room, according to the primary tasks that we perform in them. Each type of light is characterized by its own mood and functional value.

Light can be used to create rooms that visually intrigue us and enhance our everyday lives. Interior light falls into three categories: general, task and accent. The most appealing room schemes use a variety of sources to create a balanced mix of lighting types.

General lighting, also referred to as ambient and background lighting, provides comfortable background illumination. The best type of general lighting is glare-free indirect lighting, which bounces off walls and ceilings. It should be evenly distributed, with no ultrabright or shadowy spots. General light sources, such as recessed or track fixtures, should be flexible enough to suit a room's diverse needs. For example, installing a dimmer switch in a dining room allows you to soften the mood for intimate occasions or entertaining. Recessed downlighters provide the best and most effective general lighting for the living room.

The primary function of ambient or general lighting is to ensure safety and allow us to move about a room easily. Once your general lighting plan has been established you can use other types of lighting to brighten work areas, enhance color, spark drama, add interest, change moods, warm up large spaces and make small rooms appear larger.

Glass block can be used to produce some dramatic lighting effects. It allows sunlight to enter the room, but has just enough distortion to maintain privacy.

Task lighting provides essential illumination for specific jobs like writing, reading, grooming, cooking, computer work or hobbies. Task lighting, such as floor lamps, desk lamps, bedside reading lamps or countertop illumination is localized, shadow-free and easy on the eyes.

Accent lighting is purely decorative and usually used with a combination of other lighting sources, such as floor-based uplights, sconces or spotlights. Accent lighting is used to highlight a room's appealing aspects, such as artwork, collectibles, vignettes or architecture.

Natural light, such as windows and skylights, is perfect for small spaces with little natural light. Skylights, clerestory and other types of accent windows create an always-changing pattern of sunlight. Skylights lighten the mood of the room. In bedrooms, skylights not only let in natural light during the day, they also create a romantic atmosphere at night. Skylights can also create a focal point within a space.

Windows can dramatically change the sense of space in a room. Even a small amount of natural light can completely alter the look of a space. An entire wall of windows seems to eliminate the boundaries between inside and out, and increase the sense of space in the room. A glass block wall is another creative solution, letting natural light in and still preserving privacy.

In between natural and artificial lighting is candlelight. Candlelight is the most romantic kind of lighting. This also applies to oil lamps and lanterns. Many times, artificial light emulates natural light as with downlights, which produce shafts of light that resemble sunlight coming through a window.

A combination of floor and desk lamps pulls double duty in this contemporary setting. They function as task lights and also provide ample general lighting when reflected off the ceilings and walls.

Design
AMBIENT LIGHTING

Ambient light is all around us. It is the light of an overcast sky where the clouds diffuse the sun's rays. It comes from a subtle source of light and creates very little shadow. The most obvious example of ambient light is that given off by a fluorescent strip or light housed in an opaque uplight, which hides the light source. It lights the ceiling, which acts as a giant reflector, as if it were made of glass and lit from behind.

To create a comfortable ambient setting there are some important factors to consider; first is the type of light fixtures you choose. Some are very directional, like downlighting spotlights, wall sconces or table lamps, concentrating a high illumination in one area. The other factor is reflectance. Different surfaces reflect differing amounts of light. A matte-white painted plaster wall will reflect 70% of the light hitting it, absorbing the other 30%, while a dark granite or stone floor will absorb a staggering 90% of the light hitting it.

Wallwashers, such as uplighting wall sconces, are good sources of ambient lighting; they illuminate a wall and bring it into play as a reflector. The effect is extremely calming and neutral, since there is no glare to offend the eye.

*(right) **A traditional table lamp** with a pleated shade provides a soft ambient light for this quiet setting. Natural firelight supplements the lamp's illumination.*

*(opposite page) **A brass table lamp** fills this bedroom with subtle background light.*

Photo courtesy of Cy DeCosse Inc.

15

The beauty of light *refracting throughout a crystal chandelier creates an ambient light that is breathtakingly beautiful.*

Light can be shaped into many forms. An unusually large round window is the main source of ambient light during the day. Two tall floor lamps add to the ambience after the sun sets. They are adjustable and can be positioned with the light directed as desired.

Photo courtesy of Interlubke, North America

DESIGN

Ambient lighting

Ambient light creates the background light that establishes a room's character. It is essential that the living room, kitchen and family room have sufficient background light for activities such as reading, dining and watching television.

One of the primary features of ambient or background light is that it is indirect; most of the light bounces off the ceiling, walls and floor. For bounced light to be effective, the walls and ceiling must be highly reflective. White or light surfaces reflect much more light than a dark matte surface.

Ambient light sources should always be dimmable and as discreet and subtle as possible. Even a large lamp shade can produce an attractive and effective ambient light source.

With ambient light, the source is often hidden and the light cast over a wide area. Concealing the light source is another effective way to create restful background lighting. Paper shades and screens filter both daylight and artificial light. They combine both ambient and decorative lighting effects.

You can also create subtle ambient lighting by diffusing pendant lights and lamps and by redirecting an adjustable task light toward the ceiling or walls. Some fittings, such as torchière-style uplighter lamps, are designed specifically to provide indirect light.

Ambient lighting should also bring out the visual characteristics of an interior and accent the furnishings and architecture.

Ceiling-mounted track lights are directed to highlight special pieces of art displayed on the wall and shelves.

Design
ACCENT LIGHTING

Accent lighting, also referred to as display lighting or spot lighting, adds interest and draws attention to special features such as decorative displays or architectural elements.

Accent lighting focuses on a single area and can be achieved by using directional spotlighting, a table lamp with an opaque shade or an incandescent strip light mounted inside a glass-front bookcase or cabinet.

While ambient light flattens the overall look of a room, accent lighting brings out the details and points of interest. Low-voltage halogen lighting is particularly suited to accent lighting. It produces a white light that contrasts well in an overall warm ambient setting, and it has a small and bright light source that casts crisp shadows—particularly useful for spotlighting objects.

Incandescent strip lights, mounted inside this glass-front cabinet, are especially effective for adding sparkle to glassware.

18

Accent lighting

Accent lighting can also help balance light from other sources by reducing the amount of contrast in a room or illuminating dark corners and side walls. Different materials, such as glass, wood and leather, require different kinds of lighting to bring out their best qualities. Glass, for example, emits a beautiful glow when lit from above, below or behind, while ceramic, wood and leather have better color, texture and grain when lit from the top or from the front. Narrow-beam spotlights create sparkles on silver, jewelry or cut glass.

Rooms that incorporate accent lighting the most are the dining and living rooms, where the room's architecture, coloring and artwork are most often seen. If you have a strong architectural feature in any room, accent lighting is the best way to highlight it.

(photo above) **Three ceiling-mounted spotlights** *are directed toward the wall to illuminate and highlight a feature piece of art. Each of the lights can be directed independently to focus on different features, if desired.*

(photo left) **A decorative brass** *wall-mounted uplighter adds an accent of warm light and illuminates the tall ceiling. With the light directed upward, the interesting architecture becomes a focal point.*

Eyeball spotlights, *mounted on the ceiling, are directed at the bookcase to highlight an eclectic array of items. The spotlights also provide general lighting for the rest of the room.*

Design
TASK LIGHTING

Good task lighting helps us see better, avoid tired eyes and keep focused on the job at hand. Around the home we need optimum task lighting in the kitchen, bathroom, family room and bedroom for safety and convenience.

(below) **Recessed ceiling lights** *and directional track lighting provide an ample amount of task lighting for this contemporary kitchen. A set of clerestory windows, mounted high on the wall, fills the vaulted ceiling with natural light.*

Photo courtesy of Lindal Cedar Homes, Inc., Seattle, Washington

*A **counterweighted task light** provides a bright, directed source of light for the desktop area. The design uses pivoted arms with a hood at one end and a counterweight at the other for adjustability and balance.*

Wall lights *above the mirror provide task light for applying makeup and personal preparation. The glass block reflects artificial light and lets in natural light, making the most of outside light without compromising privacy.*

An array of eyeball spotlights is mounted in the ceiling and directed as needed in this multifunctional dressing room/closet area. The spotlights can be directed independently of each other to provide task lighting to a number of areas at once.

DESIGN

Task lighting

Task lights that are too bright produce a glare that tires the eyes and makes it hard for them to adjust to the level of light thrown onto the task itself. For activities such as working in the kitchen or applying makeup in the bathroom, a general background of ambient light will reduce shadows and help throw light into dark corners, cupboards and shelves.

When you are watching television or working at a computer screen, the task itself emits light. A strong background level of ambient light is all that is necessary for these situations.

As with accent lighting, the fixtures that provide task lighting should cast the light in a particular direction. The important difference between the two is that with task lighting the actual sources, the bulbs themselves, should never be seen. Any task light should have a reflective shield and should be mounted in an opaque reflector or covered with a shade to eliminate glare. Ceiling-mounted spots give a nonglare supply of ambient light by being pointed away onto the wall.

Photo courtesy of Wildwood Lamps

The woodland theme in this rustic den creates the perfect setting for this ceramic rabbit lamp. A soft fabric shade diffuses bright light and provides a comfortable light to read by.

A decorative floor lamp uses two folded paper fans to create a unique lamp shade. The white paper creates a soft, diffused light and a look similar to frosted glass. A coordinating black table lamp, with the same unusual accordion-style design, is directed up toward a piece of art hanging on the wall.

Photo courtesy of Interlubke, North America

Design

DECORATIVE LIGHTING

Decorative lighting is usually a deliberate statement that becomes part of the entire decorative scheme of a room. Many architects and interior designers excel in creating interesting lighting schemes.

Decorative lighting should also be supplemented with other types of lighting, particularly ambient, because it becomes less effective when competing with too much task or accent lighting. Decorative lighting schemes often rely on a balance of discrete elements to create a complete picture.

Kinetic lighting, or "moving light," is produced by candles, lanterns, lamps and fireplaces. It also includes the flickering neon that is sometimes seen incorporated into glass block or as part of a design theme.

Cook up something special *when designing your kitchen. Glass block allows maximum light to get through, giving the room a spacious feeling. Combined with soft blue backlighting, the glass block livens up the kitchen with its own distinctive brilliance.*

Illuminated glass-block bookends *add a nice accent light to an otherwise dark bookcase.*

Design

Decorative lighting

Lighting can be used in ways that are decorative and fun as well as functional. Decorative lighting tricks can be used to create visual accents in otherwise plain rooms. Complex effects can be achieved by using colored bulbs or using special projectors to project light onto a wall. Changing the color or shape of the bulb is an easy way to create a special lighting effect.

The most effective lighting schemes take advantage of light sources that are functional but also have a decorative impact on a setting. Chandeliers are traditional examples of decorative lighting that also provide general ambient lighting. The cut glass surfaces transform light into myriad sparkling images.

Decorative lighting can make the most of any display and bring out the natural beauty of materials such as glass, stone, ceramic and living foliage. Track-mounted spotlights can also play a decorative role when artfully positioned and directed.

(above) **A lighted glass-top table** is a special lighting effect that's easily created by placing a lamp with a globe bulb under the table. The light adds a warm glow to the layered tablecloths of cotton and lace.

(left) **A table lamp** and wall-mounted lamp are dressed with decorative shades to embellish the cowboy theme in this child's room.

Design
OUTDOOR LIGHTING

Garden lighting brings out the special beauty of your yard or garden at night and increases the amount of time you can enjoy an outdoor setting. It allows you to illuminate your favorite features, keeping those you wish to conceal in the dark. Well-designed outdoor lighting can make a small garden seem larger and more spacious, and large gardens seem smaller and more intimate.

Outdoor lighting fixtures must be weather-proof, durable and easy to maintain. Common materials used for outdoor lighting are aluminum, stainless steel, shatterproof glass or plastic. Types of outdoor lighting include: wall lights, flood-lights, path lights, accent lights and special lighting for pools and fountains.

Special features *become spectacular with a little outdoor illumination.*

Photo courtesy of Bachman's Landscaping Service. Sue Hartley, Photography

Photo courtesy of Intermatic Inc.

Photo (bottom) courtesy of Lindal Cedar Homes, Inc., Seattle, Washington

*A **combination of outdoor fixtures** illuminates various areas of interest in this outdoor setting. Low area lights spotlight special planting areas, while the waterfall in the pond is featured by using an underwater fixture. (inset) **Even from the outside looking in,** interior lighting becomes part of the outdoor lighting scheme, creating a spectacular effect.*

Outdoor lighting

Outdoor lighting should be as nonglaring as possible. Most exterior fittings are designed for use with low-wattage lamps or have antiglare attachments, such as baffles or louvers.

A number of different techniques can be used in an outdoor lighting scheme, such as downlighting, uplighting, area lighting, moonlighting, spotlighting, accent lighting, shadowing, contour lighting and fill lighting. The differences are found in the position of the light source and the direction of the light.

These outdoor lighting techniques can be used to highlight a specific landscape feature, such as a tree or fountain, and add a soft ambient background light or a whimsical sparkle of decorative light.

Underwater lighting *can be used to create dramatic effects that become even more spectacular when combined with strategically placed spotlights.*

Photo courtesy of Rockscapes Lighting Inc.

Decorative downlighters *line this sandy path, providing a lovely view during the day and a well-lit walkway at night.*

Both bottom photos courtesy of Intermatic Inc.

An intricate outdoor lighting system *defines the perimeter of the yard and highlights various planting areas. Uplighting next to the house illuminates the interesting texture on the outside of the home.*

PORTFOLIO OF LIGHTS

Today's market offers an array of exciting and innovative light sources to choose from. There's a lighting solution for almost every situation. The choice of light sources ranges from the familiar filament bulb to contemporary sources, such as fluorescent and halogen bulbs. This section of the book profiles some of the most commonly used and popular types of fixtures, such as table lamps, wall lights, spotlights, chandeliers and floor lights. Also included are ideas for natural light, outdoor lighting and some interesting and unique decorative lighting ideas.

Cost and quality of light are two important factors to consider when deciding what types of light sources to include in your lighting plan. It is also important that the type of bulb you choose is physically compatible with the matching fixture.

A fixture is as important to the overall lighting scheme as the light source itself. The fitting holds the light source, or bulb, in place and directs and controls the flow of light. Often it is the fixture that shapes the light and determines the impact it has. The physical characteristics of a fixture should also coordinate with the overall design theme of the room.

Paper lantern-style table lamp.
Photo courtesy of Cy DeCosse Inc.

Strauss crystal chandelier.
Photo courtesy of Schonbek Worldwide Lighting Inc.

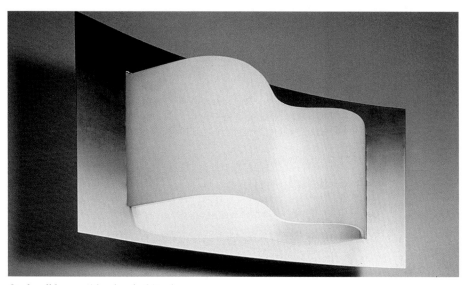

Steel wall lamp, with colored white glass.
Photo courtesy of Leucos Lighting

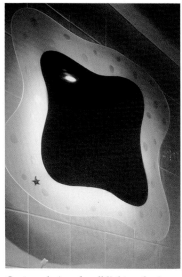

Custom-designed wall light and mirror.
Photo courtesy of Amtico Company Limited

Colored glass uplighting table lamps.
Photo courtesy of Leucos Lighting

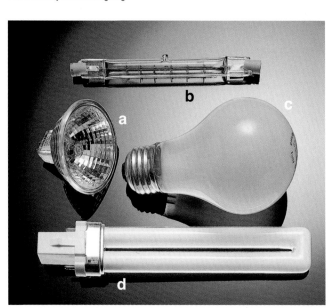

Common bulbs *include halogen bulbs, with reflectors (a); and without reflectors (b); incandescent bulbs (c); and compact fluorescent bulbs (d).*
Photo courtesy of Cy DeCosse Inc.

Torchière floor lamp.
Photo courtesy of Cy DeCosse Inc.

Table lights

Table lamps often must perform several functions within a lighting scheme. They can act as task lights for visually demanding functions like reading, provide general ambient lighting in a room and help reinforce an interior design theme or atmosphere.

The popular image of a table lamp is a decorative base with a socket for a bulb and a detachable shade. With new technology in light sources and materials changing every day, the range of table lamps you have to choose from is growing considerably. The portfolio of lights section features examples of some of the most popular and clever designs in table lamps today.

Pure polished brass carriage lamp.
Photo courtesy of Frederick Cooper Lamps

Pure antique brass & black candlestick lamp.
Photo courtesy of Frederick Cooper Lamps

Verdi Fountain table torchière
Photo courtesy of Wildwood Lamps

China Today lamp
Photo courtesy of Wildwood Lamps

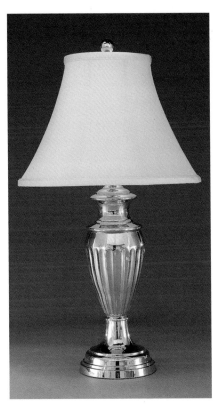

Fluted urn lamp
Photo courtesy of Wildwood Lamps

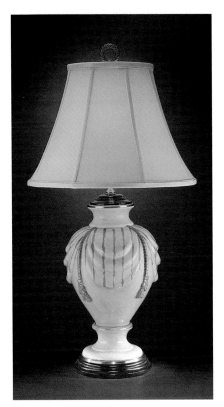

Pinstripes & tassels lamp
Photo courtesy of Wildwood Lamps

Green wood candlestick with brown accents
Photo courtesy of Frederick Cooper Lamps

Italian ceramic table lamp
Photo courtesy of Frederick Cooper Lamps

Urn with roses table lamp
Photo courtesy of Wildwood Lamps

Table lights

Acanthus vase lamp
Photo courtesy of Wildwood Lamps

Colored glass uplighting table lamps
Photo courtesy of Leucos Lighting

Rain Forest themed table lamp
Photo courtesy of Frederick Cooper Lamps

Veggie parrot lamp
Photo courtesy of Wildwood Lamps

Custom-designed lamp, made from a vase
Photo courtesy of Cy DeCosse Inc.

Sun & Moon medallian lamp
Photo courtesy of Wildwood Lamps

Old world map rectangular table lamp
Photo courtesy of Frederick Cooper Lamps

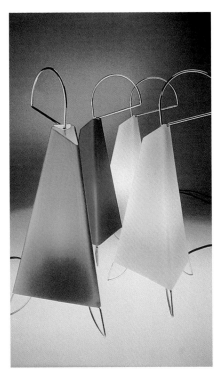

Triangular blown glass table lamps
Photo courtesy of Leucos Lighting

Tang horse lamp
Photo courtesy of Wildwood Lamps

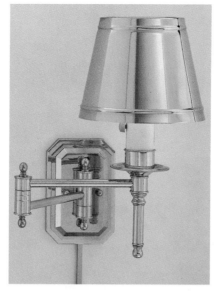

Brass swing-arm lamp
Photo courtesy of Cassella lighting

Pure cast aged brass antique sconces
Photo courtesy of Frederick Cooper Lamps

Wall lights

Wall lights offer the widest variety of design and effect of any type of modern lighting available today. Wall lighting maximizes the impact of light as a design tool by using the flat surface of the wall to create a range of effects, from soft, diffused ambient light, to extremely localized spotlighting.

Antique brass sconce
Photo courtesy of Frederick Cooper Lamps

Cylinder-style micro sconce
Photo courtesy of Cassella lighting

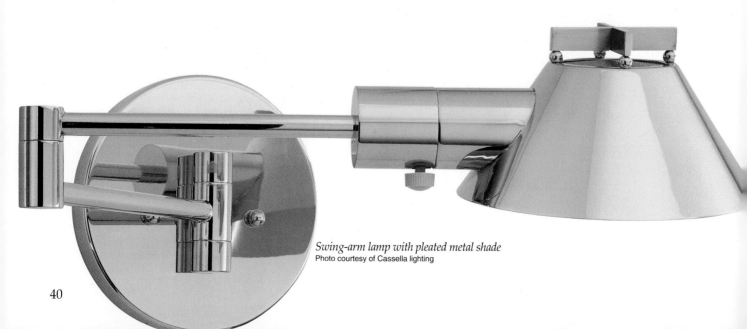

Swing-arm lamp with pleated metal shade
Photo courtesy of Cassella lighting

Iron and crystal sconce
Photo courtesy of Niermann Weeks

Louis XVI sconce
Photo courtesy of Niermann Weeks

Alabaster wall wash
Photo courtesy of Wildwood Lamps

Gothic tole sconce
Photo courtesy of Niermann Weeks

White glass wall sconce in "Volo" design
Photo courtesy of Leucos Lighting

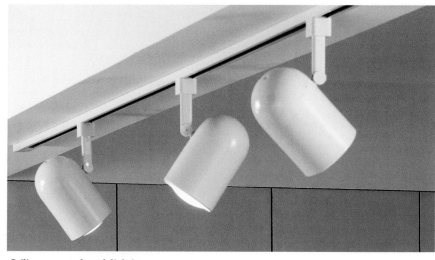

Ceiling-mounted track lighting
Photo courtesy of Congoleum Corporation

Ceiling lights & chandeliers

Until recently ceiling lights, also called pendant lights, were criticized for their unflattering visual effects. New styles and clever developments in the quality and ability to control the light from these fixtures have overcome these previous problems.

Decorative chandeliers are a type of pendant light that is often used in antique or period theme design schemes. Their prominent central location on the ceiling gives these lights a strong impact on a room.

Contemporary hanging ceiling lights
Photo courtesy of Interlubke, North America

Directional track lighting
Photo courtesy of Homes by Timberpeg

Fluorescent ceiling fixture
Photo courtesy of Amtico International

Trilliane Strass crystal chandelier
Photo courtesy of Schonbek Worldwide Lighting Inc.

Venetian lantern
Photo courtesy of Niermann Weeks

Rivoli chandelier
Photo courtesy of Niermann Weeks

Hand-cut crystal chandelier
Photo courtesy of Schonbek Worldwide Lighting Inc.

Iron & crystal chandelier
Photo courtesy of Niermann Weeks

Strass crystal chandelier
Photo courtesy of Schonbek Worldwide Lighting Inc.

Floor lamps

Floor lamps offer a range of lighting options, from ambient background light to task lighting. Floor lamps provide as much general light as a ceiling-mounted pendant light but since they plug into the wall they require no extra wiring and are extremely portable. Because height and direction of light is often adjustable, floor lights are a more flexible option than a lighting scheme that involves wall lights and table lamps.

The traditional brass floor lamp, with its pleated shade, represents the image of the conventional standard floor lamp. A more contemporary version of the floor lamp would be the popular halogen torchière lamp.

Brass floor lamp
Photo courtesy of Cassella lighting

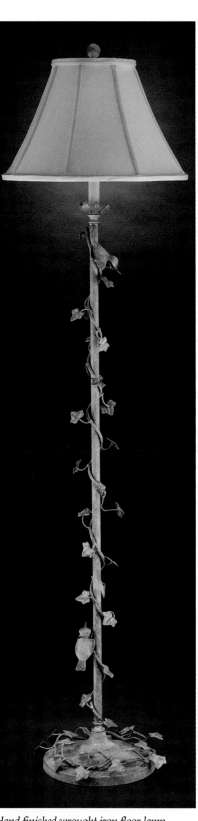

Hand finished wrought iron floor lamp
Photo courtesy of Wildwood Lamps

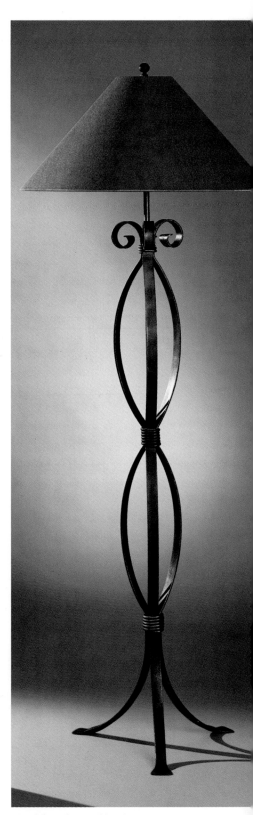

Hand-forged iron ribbon lamps
Photo courtesy of Frederick Cooper Lamps

Solid mahogany twin-arm oil lamp
Photo courtesy of Frederick Cooper Lamps

Antique brass art déco torchière lamp
Photo courtesy of Frederick Cooper Lamps

Leaf tripod floor lamp
Photo courtesy of Wildwood Lamps

Natural & kinetic light

When designing a lighting scheme for your home, remember that it must supplement and complement the natural light that a room receives. Sources of natural light, such as windows, skylights and patio doors, not only allow natural light to illuminate a room, they also expand the sense of space in a room by removing the solid barriers created by the ceiling and walls.

Kinetic or moving light can be found in the form of candles, lanterns and fireplaces. This type of natural light creates a soft, warm light and enhances the romantic ambience of a setting.

Glass block brightens the room with natural light.
Photo courtesy of Pittsburgh Corning

Glass block wall illuminates the entire office with natural light.
Photo courtesy of Interlubke, North America

Skylights in a vaulted ceiling let in natural light.
Photo courtesy of Crestline

Tall casement windows fill a room with natural light.
Photo courtesy of Crestline

Finished- iron candelabras
Photo courtesy of Wildwood Lamps

Six-candle candelabra
Photo courtesy of Cy DeCosse Inc.

Baroque sconce
Photo courtesy of Niermann Weeks

A glassed-in atrium lets in natural light.
Photo courtesy of Lindal Cedar Homes, Inc., Seattle, Washington

Wall sconce with traditional candles
Photo courtesy of Cy DeCosse Inc.

Outdoor lighting

Outdoor lighting lets you enjoy the unique beauty of a deck at night. Lighting will also expand the usefulness of a deck to include nighttime activities. Well-planned outdoor lighting focuses on the best features of the deck and leaves those you wish to conceal in the dark.

A well-designed lighting plan can shape the view and mood of any outdoor environment. With the proper lighting effects, you can make a small deck seem larger and more spacious, or an expansive deck smaller and more intimate.

Outdoor lighting fills an area with light and helps indicate where railings, steps, level changes or other possible hazards might be. It also discourages intruders by illuminating the area and eliminating shadows near the house. Lighting allows you to use the deck after dark for many activities, from relaxing to entertaining.

Many lighting techniques can be applied to an outdoor lighting scheme. The differences are in the position of the light source and whether it is aimed up, down or across a surface. Use a combination of lighting techniques to bring light to different parts of your deck and link it with the rest of your outdoor lighting.

Downlighting is a general term that involves the lighting of an object from above and is often used to describe a number of lighting techniques, including spotlighting, accent lighting or contour lighting. Uplighting is another general term referring to lighting something from below. Shadowing, mirror lighting and silhouetting are examples of uplighting. Safety is another important reason for outdoor lighting on a deck. It directs users where to walk and allows people to feel more comfortable on the deck.

Standing spot-light
Photo courtesy of Rockscapes

Lantern fixture
Photo courtesy of Rockscapes

Standard tier light
Photo courtesy of Rockscapes

Rectangular flood-light
Photo courtesy of Intermatic Inc.

Low-profile brick light
Photo courtesy of Intermatic Inc.

Low-profile edge light
Photo courtesy of Intermatic Inc.

Post light
Photo courtesy of Idaho Wood

Decorative yard lamp
Photo courtesy of Rockscapes

Wrought-iron lantern
Photo courtesy of Rockscapes

Well light
Photo courtesy of Intermatic Inc.

Flare light
Photo courtesy of Intermatic Inc.

Tier light
Photo courtesy of Intermatic Inc.

A PORTFOLIO OF
LIGHTING
IDEAS

Photo courtesy of Schonbek Worldwide Lighting Inc.

HALLWAY & ENTRY LIGHTING

Hallways and entryways present many unique lighting challenges. Because these areas are by design quite conspicuous, they call for lighting that flatters and enhances their positive characteristics.

In many cases the front entryway provides the first impression for the home. The style and character of the house should be illuminated to offer a hearty welcome to visitors without subjecting them to a harsh, glaring transition from the outdoors to the indoors.

A hallway's open space makes good lighting an absolute necessity. With the proper lighting scheme, blank spaces are downplayed while color and architectural design are accentuated and showcased. Hallways are also frequently used to display paintings or sculpture, which are highlighted by good lighting design. With some intelligent planning, a hallway can become a truly theatrical area in which to display your favorite artwork or create a very distinct mood for your home.

From the standpoint of practicality, lighting is of utmost importance in hallways and entryways. These areas are busy with traffic and must be well lighted to ensure safety, particularly around stairways. Front hall closets, locked doors and misplaced keys become real headaches without adequate lighting, so be sure to incorporate a subtle, yet effective lighting scheme when planning or refurbishing your home's hallways and entryways.

The soft, warm light of this entryway offers a soothing welcome to any house guests. The overhead light is dispersed throughout the area by the translucent glass walls, which allow the light to penetrate while offering solid room separation.

These glass railings enhance the bright lighting scheme in this front hall stairway, drawing attention upward, like the stairs themselves.

Photo courtesy of Lindal Cedar Homes, Inc., Seattle, Washington

Photo courtesy of Grange

(above) **Sometimes the best lighting** is natural. This backyard entryway opens directly into the kitchen and family room, and the entire space is filled with natural sunlight from the windows to keep these well-used areas bright.

(left) **This bright window** pours light on what would otherwise be a dark, dreary entrance stairway, adding fresh, well-needed natural light to the area.

Photo courtesy of Wildwood Lamps

LIVING & DINING ROOM LIGHTING

Living rooms and dining rooms are usually filled with lighting options. The style and purpose of these rooms differ from individual to individual and from family to family. Keep the lighting for these areas flexible and effective; your activities in living rooms and dining rooms are many and diverse.

The lighting in a dining room is often focused on the table, with supplementary lighting around the edges of the room to create a relaxed, enjoyable dining atmosphere. Choose lighting schemes that will accommodate both intimate formal dinners and simple family meals.

In traditional living rooms, lamps are often used to create pockets of light at various positions throughout the area. This lighting style is relaxing and creates boundaries for different activities and interests. In addition, distinct islands of light counteract deep shadows in drapes or furniture to vary the visual image and break up a glaring, overly bright room.

To create a conversational mood, you might want to consider a softer, more evenly distributed lighting scheme in your living room. Whatever your personal tastes, remember that most rooms benefit greatly from contrasting shadows and light. Even in the most modern rooms, you should vary the light tones for a pleasant, relaxing atmosphere.

Living rooms and dining rooms often showcase interesting architectural features or prized artwork. Plan your lighting to accentuate these features and highlight the positive qualities of the room. Soft, indirect lighting, for example, would probably be best for a room with a spectacular outdoor view, while more precisely directed lighting would draw attention to specific room characteristics such as paintings, furniture or wall texture. Determine the strengths and weaknesses of your living room or dining room before deciding on the lighting design that best suits your needs.

Photo courtesy of Homes by Timberpeg; Ross Chapple, Photographer

During the day natural window lighting emphasizes the openess of this beautiful dining room. At night the single fixture casts dramatic shadows on the vaulted ceilings while focusing light upon the meal.

A beam of light from an overhead wall fixture shines light on this pleasant living room nook, creating an island for relaxation and reading. During the day, the window provides a beautiful view and much needed light.

(above) **The general illumination** *for these rooms is provided by the shaded window. The lighting design is accented by a modern pendant and floor standing lamp.*

(left) **The classic mood** *of this room is emphasized by the open atmosphere created by the large windows and high ceiling.*

61

(above) **The conversational mood** *of this living room is fostered by the bright overall lighting scheme, while individual lamps make isolated areas of concentration a realistic option.*

(right) **A centrally located fixture** *distributes light evenly throughout the room and casts interesting shadows in corners and on drapes.*

***Highlight outstanding** architectural or artistic features by focusing small downlights on the area of interest. This lighting scheme consists of individual lighting stations rather than a unified central source.*

Candlelight *has always been a dining room favorite because of the warm, traditional glow it lends a room. Supplementary lights along the walls accentuate the wall texture and bring attention to the artwork.*

A delicate overhead fixture complements the room design with simple grace and charm. Wall fixtures help to distribute light evenly around the room.

Photo courtesy of Lindal Cedar Homes, Inc., Seattle, Washington

For traditional elegance, nothing can compete with a grand dining room chandelier, which provides textured light and a beautiful dining room feature.

Photo courtesy of Crestline

Photo courtesy of Cy DeCosse Inc.

65

Photo courtesy of Homes by Timberpeg ; R. Lear Design, Ross Chapple, Photographer

KITCHEN LIGHTING

Perhaps the most versatile room in the home, the kitchen is often much more than a place to prepare food. From informal dining room to family meeting center, the kitchen serves many roles and could be considered the most important room in the house. The lighting scheme for your kitchen should be suitable for the many activities that take place there.

Natural light is usually prominent in the kitchen. However, kitchens are very often utilized after dark, making good artificial lighting an absolute necessity. Thankfully, because of extensive counter and cupboard space in most kitchens, unobtrusive lighting can be accomplished without extensive glare or clutter.

Of course, safety is a primary concern in the kitchen. Many burns, cuts and scrapes can result from inadequate lighting. Because the cooking process will sometimes range over the entire room with many tasks taking place at once, it is extremely important to keep the entire work area well lighted and safe. A kitchen with good lighting makes cooking a fun activity, rather than a dark, dreary chore.

Many kitchen lighting designs provide a subtle transition from cooking areas to social space. Away from the main work area, concealed over-the-counter lighting gives way to more direct overhead fixtures, perfect for conversation or dining. How you choose to accomplish this transition depends on your kitchen design, and your own personal tastes.

Great natural lighting is a common element in kitchens, but specific task lighting, like the overhead pendant light and recessed fixtures above, is a necessity when preparing food or cleaning up.

Track lighting *is particularly useful in a kitchen, where specific cooking tasks call for focused beams of bright light from above.*

(above) **Style combines with function** with these three hanging pendants. They illuminate the countertop while perfectly matching the kitchen decor.

(left) **The transition from kitchen** to dining room is smooth and seamless with the gentle illumination of the stovetop light combining with two delicate, but effective, counter pendants. The dining room fixture completes the lighting scheme.

69

Photo courtesy of Homes by Timberpeg; Kevin Ruedisueli, Arch., Neil Steinberg, Photographer

(above) **A quartet** *of overhead fixtures fully illuminates the kitchen worksurface while remaining unobtrusive.*

(right) **The kitchen's small,** *direct track lights provide an interesting contrast to the huge pendant light over the dining table, which throws a soft glow over the entire eating area.*

Photo courtesy of Lindal Cedar Homes, Inc., Seattle, Washington

(left) **Glass blocks** *refract the natural and artificial light and add to this kitchen's bright, open atmosphere.*

(below) **The combination** *of overhead recessed and globe lights illuminates the entire kitchen area without clutter or glare.*

Photo courtesy of GenCorp.

BEDROOM LIGHTING

Bedroom lighting presents a number of interesting challenges. Since the bedroom usually functions as a dressing room, reading room and sleeping area, the lighting design must be very diverse and flexible.

Most bedrooms contain some sort of dressing area. These areas are often overlooked, but specific task lighting should be assigned to them. Dressing tables should include a light source placed in front of the face, not behind it. Closets should also contain their own internal light source, since general room light can seldom penetrate the deep recesses of a well-stocked walk-in closet.

Bedrooms often double as studies. Whether you are reading in bed or looking over some

papers at a nearby desk, the lighting should be able to accommodate comfortable reading. Rather than opt for overhead lighting at the bed, which can lend a disturbing spotlight feel to the atmosphere, consider positioning a fixture at each side. It's also a good idea to put the lighting controls within reach of the bed for convenient late-night access.

No matter how thoroughly you plan your bedroom, the inspiration for the lighting must be more than simple practicality. Obviously, the lighting design must be able to sustain a completely relaxing, comfortable mood. Use careful consideration when choosing your bedroom lighting to avoid clumsy, uncomfortable design; create a tasteful environment that is distinctly your own.

Photo courtesy of GenCorp.

These two classic lamps match the bedroom decor and mood. Notice the decorative mirror, which is placed strategically between them for reflective effect.

Natural morning light *bathes this cozy bedroom. A convenient bedside lamp makes late reading easy, while a wrought-iron candle holder waits in the corner for a romantic evening.*

Photo courtesy of Laura Ashley

(left) **The shape of this window** spreads natural light throughout the room. The sides of the alcove feature decorative candle holders.

(below) **Good decorative lighting fixtures** match the room decor while spreading light throughout their designated areas. Here a bedside lamp is paired with a desk area reading lamp.

Photo courtesy of GenCorp.

This modern bedroom provides great storage lighting by positioning recessed ceiling lights directly in front of the wardrobe closet. The closet doors are themselves slightly reflective to add to the modern mood of the room.

*A **bedroom alcove** is perfect for reading in the sunlight. At night a fireplace lends a soothing glow to the room.*

Photo courtesy of Kohler Company

BATHROOM LIGHTING

Since bathrooms often have little, if any, natural light, the lighting scheme becomes even more important than in other areas of the house. There are two basic approaches to planning a bathroom. Some people prefer a bright environment, while others choose a darker, more intimate feeling. One thing is clear: without an interesting lighting scheme, a bathroom's atmosphere could seem extremely claustrophobic and dreary.

It is always necessary to keep the sink area thoroughly illuminated. The main focus of the bathroom is often the mirror, so plan your lighting to focus on that area. Many bathroom mirrors are fitted with lights behind or directly in front of them to make grooming and personal hygiene easier.

Because of the sink, bathtub and shower, there are safety issues involved in bathroom lighting. Plan the lighting much as you would for any other room, drawing adequate attention to significant architectural and decorative features, but remember to keep bathing and grooming areas well illuminated.

Photo courtesy of Crestline

Light pours into this bathroom from the skylight, window and mirror fixtures. The location of the skylight celebrates the tub space, the room's central feature. At night, the artificial lighting creates an intimate retreat.

Warm morning light *bathes a vintage tub in this unusual bathroom space. The sink area is served by a pair of ornate wall fixtures and a highly effective skylight.*

(above) **This wide, open** bathroom configuration allows light to spread throughout the area and highlight the outstanding architectural features.

Two bright yellow globes illuminate the sink and mirror area, often a critical lighting spot.

Many people prefer *an extremely bright, well-lighted bathroom. This room features a tub in front of well-draped windows, which allow light to enter without sacrificing privacy. The corners are crowned with antique-style wall lamps.*

Photo courtesy of Lindal Cedar Homes, Inc., Seattle, Washington

Photo this page and opposite page courtesy of Kohler Company

(above) **The shiny marble,** large mirrors and torchlike wall fixtures keep this bathroom bright and reflective while maintaining the atmosphere of an ancient Roman spa.

(left) **Most bathroom mirrors** feature some sort of dedicated task lighting to illuminate activities such as shaving or washing. These lights, combined with a nearby window, serve both a functional and decorative purpose.

Photo courtesy of Interlubke, North America

DEN & FAMILY ROOM LIGHTING

Dens and family rooms are flexible, multiuse living areas. A den can be little more than a home library, or it can be an office for someone working out of their home. Family rooms often have many functions, from entertaining guests to relaxing in front of a fireplace. With these many functions, dens and family rooms are best served by a wide variety of imaginative lighting.

Family rooms generally require a lighting scheme that will allow you to relax when reading, watching television or conversing. Concealed lights or a spotlight array often produce this relaxing effect. If you use your family room to display artwork, you will need lighting that highlights and showcases the pieces. There is a wide range of decorative lighting options for a family room, from colored bulbs to wall uplights. To keep the lighting design flexible, you might want to consider dimmer switches to brighten or darken the environment.

Dens are places of concentration. The lighting design should encourage study and work without distraction or eyestrain. This rule should be followed whether the den is traditional or modern. Avoid excessive glare, and install specific task lighting to help you focus on the work at hand.

Matching the lighting fixtures can sometimes help to unify a den or family room. This traditional den combines areas of light and deep shadow and features matching desk and wall lamps.

(*above*) **Overhead recessed bulbs** *highlight the bookshelves while a floor standing lamp allows the books to be read with a minimum of eyestrain.*

The lighting sources in this den *are positioned for efficiency and practical use, creating concentrated pools of light.*

An interesting array of accent lights focuses on the bookshelf while a sleek chair lamp provides the task lighting in this stylishly modern den.

The den and family room are combined *here with interesting results. Natural light fills the television room, while artistic floor-standing and ceiling-hung fixtures bring brightness to the room's interior.*

This simple desk light adds a decorative touch to the heavy wooden secretary in this quaint reading room.

Photo courtesy of Bachman's Landscaping Service, Sue Hartley, Photography

OUTDOOR LIGHTING

Outdoor lighting provides security and decoration for gardens, entrances, patios and pools. When done properly, a good outdoor lighting scheme creates its own mood, enhances the natural beauty of the outdoors and provides safety by illuminating your home and lawn.

You have many options when lighting a landscape. Path lighting ensures safety while providing a beautiful nightime scene. Bright spotlights against a battery of trees present a striking image that changes with each passing breeze. With the right lighting, your landscape can be enjoyed day or night.

When lighting an entrance, your goal should be to provide security while offering a friendly first impression. The entrance to your home should be welcoming and warm, with enough light to enhance the structure and draw attention to its positive aspects.

Patios and pools need good lighting to encourage nighttime use. Furthermore, these features are often enhanced by good lighting design. A well-lighted pool or patio is simply more enjoyable than a dreary and potentially dangerous setting.

Outdoor lighting is both decorative and practical. With a little imagination, the creative options are nearly endless.

Photo courtesy of Intermatic Lighting

Small ground lights decorate the yard shrubs while large globes announce the home's entrance with an understated grace and charm.

***These outdoor fixtures** mesh with the indoor lighting scheme to give the entire home the look of a giant lantern.*

(above) **A bright entrance** *flatters the home and provides valuable security.*

(below) **Pools become beautiful** *outdoor features with imaginative lighting. This yard is filled with a soft blue hue from underwater pool lights.*

Decorative outdoor lights *draw attention to prominent landscape features like pools or fountains and make the area safe for nightime usage.*

Delicate ground lanterns *create isolated pockets of interest in the backyard, adding variety and beauty to simple gardens.*

Soft incandescent lights illuminate a flagstone walkway, showing the way without excessive glare or annoying brightness.

LIST OF CONTRIBUTORS

We'd like to thank the following companies for providing the photographs used in this book:

The Amtico Company Limited
6480 Roswell Road
Atlanta, GA 30328
1-800-268-4260

Bachman's Landscaping Service
6010 Lyndale Avenue S.
Minneapolis, MN 55419
612-861-7600

Broyhill Furniture Industries, Inc.
One Broyhill Park
Lenoir, NC 28633
704-758-3111

Casella Lighting
111 Rhode Island
San Francisco, CA 94103
415-626-9600

Congoleum Corporation
3705 Quackenbridge Road-Suite 211
P.O. Box 3127
Mercerville, NJ 08619-0127
609-584-3000

Conrad Imports
575 Tenth Street
San Francisco, CA 94103-4829
415-626-3303

Crestline Windows & Doors
SNE Enterprises
One Wausau Center
Wausau, WI 54402-8007
715-845-1161

Frederick Cooper Lamps
2545 West Diversey Avenue
Chicago, IL 60647
312-384-0800

GenCorp. Wallcovering Division
Three University Plaza
Hackensack, NJ 07601
201-489-0100

Grange
200 Lexington Avenue
New York, NY 10016
1-800-GRANGE-1

Intermatic Lighting, Inc.
Intermatic Plaza
Spring Grove, IL 60081-9698
815-675-2321

Interlubke
P.O. Box 139
Athens, NY 12015
518-945-1007

Kohler Co.
444 Highland Drive
Kohler, WI 53044
414-457-4441

Laura Ashley
1-800-367-2000

LEUCOS USA INC.
70 Campus Plaza II
Edison, NJ 08837
908-225-0010

Lindal Cedar Homes, Inc.
P.O. Box 24426
Seattle, WA 98124
206-725-0900

Niermann Weeks Co.
760 Generals Highway
Millersville, MD 21108
410-923-0123

Pittsburgh Corning Corp.
800 Presque Isle Drive
Pittsburgh, PA 15239-2799
412-327-6100

Rockscapes Lighting, Inc.
419 Larchmont Boulevard, #68
Los Angeles, CA 90004
1-800-469-3637

Schonbek Worldwide Lighting, Inc.
61 Industrial Boulevard
Plattsburgh, NY 12901
513-563-7500

Timberpeg
P.O. Box 5474
West Lebanon, NH 03784
603-298-8820

Tyndale, a division of Frederick Cooper
2545 West Diversey Avenue
Chicago, IL 60647
312-384-0800

Wildwood Lamps
419 Edgedale Drive
High Point, NC 27262
910-885-4858